Rooted In The Call

Rooted In The Call

A chairperson's Guide to Spirit-Led Leadership and Discernment

Keith Clark-Hoyos

Rooted in the Call

A Chairperson's Guide to Spirit-Led Discernment

Copyright © 2025 Keith Clark-Hoyos

All rights reserved. No part of this book may be reproduced in any form or by any means, electronic or mechanical, including photocopying, recording, or by any information storage and retrieval system, without the prior written permission of the publisher, except in the case of brief quotations embodied in critical articles and reviews.

Scripture quotations are taken from the following translations:

- New Revised Standard Version Updated Edition (NRSVue), © 2021 National Council of the Churches of Christ in the United States of America. Used by permission. All rights reserved.
- Contemporary English Version (CEV), © 1991, 1992, 1995 by American Bible Society. Used by permission. All rights reserved.
- New International Version (NIV), © 1973, 1978, 1984, 2011 by Biblica, Inc.™ Used by permission. All rights reserved worldwide.
- Common English Bible (CEB), © 2011 Common English Bible. Used by permission. All rights reserved worldwide.
- The Living Bible (TLB), © 1971 by Tyndale House Foundation. Used by permission. All rights reserved.
- The Message (MSG), © 1993, 2002, 2018 by Eugene H. Peterson. Used by permission. All rights reserved.

Printed in the United States of America.

ISBN: 979-8-9987673-7-1

Cover design: Keith Clark-Hoyos
Interior design: Keith Clark-Hoyos

Published by Clark-Hoyos Publications
Topeka, KS

For more resources, visit:
www.ChurchTrainingCenter.com

To the dedicated individuals who are willing to step into leadership for their church,
who answer the Spirit's call to guide with discernment, courage, and humility.
Your willingness to serve nurtures roots of faith, strengthens communities,
and helps the Church grow in alignment with God's mission.

And to my wife, partner, and best friend, Zulima, who walks beside me in this calling, supports me in the work,
and seeks the Spirit's guidance with me, so that together we may remain rooted in the life God has entrusted to us.

Books by Keith Clark-Hoyos

Called Together: A Spirit-Led Discernment Guide for Congregational Planning

Embracing Our Call: A Practical Guide for Church Governing Body Leaders

The Ministry of Money: A Treasurer's Role in the Mission of the Church

Serving the Call: A Hands-On Workbook for Faithful Church Boards

Sacred Listening: Discovering God's Call for Your Life

The Heart of Stewardship, The Practice of Faith

Rooted in the Call: A Chairperson's Guide to Spirit-Led Leadership and Discernment

About the Author

Keith Clark-Hoyos is a dedicated leader known for his unwavering positivity and remarkable ability to guide and inspire within the realm of church leadership and administration. His life journey has been characterized by a deep commitment to personal and professional growth, a passion for teaching and coaching, and a profound love for nurturing individuals and organizations toward their highest potential.

In 2015, Keith transitioned from his role as a church judicatory leader to found Church Training Center — a thriving consulting, coaching, training, and accounting firm serving churches and nonprofits across the nation. Together with his wife and partner, he has built a team that supports mission-driven ministries with clarity, care, and Spirit-led wisdom.

Keith holds a Master of Arts in Ministry, Leadership & Service from Claremont School of Theology and an undergraduate degree in Business Administration and Church Ministries from Simpson University. He is also a Daoist Monk in the Wù Zhēn Pài (Awakened Reality Sect) lineage and brings a deeply contemplative and spiritually grounded presence to his work.

At the heart of Keith's calling is a desire to empower church leaders to live faithfully, lead effectively, and align all resources — financial, human, and spiritual — with the mission God has placed before them.

Table of Contents

Table of Contents
Introduction: The Call of the Mission Keeper — 1
Part I: The Sacred Role of Chairperson — 7
    Chapter 1 – Planted by the Spirit — 9
    Chapter 2 – Roots of Leadership — 15
Part II: Leading with Discernment — 21
    Chapter 3 – Shaping the Agenda — 23
    Chapter 4 – Listening for the Spirit — 29
    Chapter 5 – Facilitating Dialogue — 35
Part III: Anchoring in Mission — 41
    Chapter 6 – Policy to Practice — 43
    Chapter 7 – Rhythm of the Year — 49
    Chapter 8 – Nurturing the Whole Body — 55
Part IV: Remaining Rooted — 61
    Chapter 9 – Crisis and Change — 63
    Chapter 10 – Succession — 69
    Chapter 11 – Rule of Life — 75
    Chapter 12 – Rooted for the Future — 81
Conclusion — 87
10 Practices of Spirit-Led Chairing — 93
Scripture Index — 97
Effective Church Leadership Community — 99
Continue the Journey — 101
A Final Word — 103

Introduction: The Call of the Mission Keeper

Welcome, and thank you.

By saying yes to the call of chairing your church's governing body, you have stepped into one of the most crucial and sacred leadership roles in the life of the church. It is not a role that many seek, yet it is one that shapes the health, mission, and witness of the congregation in profound ways. Your willingness to serve in this way is itself an act of discipleship. You have placed your gifts, your presence, and your energy before God, trusting that they will be used to sustain and guide the body. For that courage, I offer you my gratitude.

Too often, the chairperson is imagined simply as the "manager" of meetings, the one tasked with keeping people on time and on topic. While that is part of the work, it does not capture the heart of this role. In truth, you are much more. You are the one who helps ensure that the governing body remains rooted in its calling. You are the one who steadies the soil so that discernment can grow. You are the one entrusted with helping the board see the larger picture when the weeds of details threaten to overwhelm.

In the language I often share with church leaders, you are the **Mission Keeper**.

The Mission Keeper's sacred task is to guide the governing body so that the church's calling has been discerned and confirmed—and then to ensure that all of the energy and resources of the congregation are directed toward that calling. Like roots that hold a tree steady through wind and drought, you hold the board steady, continually returning it to the question: *Does this reflect what God is calling us to do and to be?*

You do not carry this burden alone. The church's leadership is shared, woven together in a holy partnership of distinct but complementary roles.

The pastor is the **Vision Driver**. Even if a pastor does not see themselves as naturally visionary, they are entrusted with guiding the church toward its future in God's care. The Vision Driver helps the body glimpse what God is calling it to become, pointing toward a future where today's seeds will bear fruit. They remind the congregation that God's Spirit is not finished shaping them, but is leading them into new seasons of growth.

The treasurer is the **Mission Interpreter**. They take what can feel like numbers on a page and help the board see those numbers as testimony. The budget and financial reports are not only technical records—they tell a story of faithfulness, showing how resources are being used to fulfill mission. The Mission Interpreter helps the governing body read those numbers not as limits, but as mirrors, revealing how the church is—or is not—living into its calling.

Mission Keeper, Vision Driver, Mission Interpreter.

When these three roles are aligned, leadership becomes balanced and Spirit-led. The board does not get lost in details without direction. It does not rush into visions unmoored from resources. It does not manage money apart from mission. Together, these roles form a steady partnership that holds the congregation in its true purpose: to glorify God and to serve faithfully in its community.

As chairperson, your place within this partnership is essential. You are not expected to know everything, to solve every problem, or to carry the church on your shoulders. Rather, you are called to keep the board focused on its mission, to hold space for discernment, and to remind the body of its sacred role. You are the one who ensures that time, energy, and attention are given to listening for the Spirit's leading.

This book has been written to accompany you in that calling.

Throughout these chapters, you will find both reflection and practice. There will be moments that invite you to pause and pray, questions to help you discern, and tools to guide your leadership. You will meet fictionalized stories of churches that wrestled with decisions, seasons, and challenges, and you will see how Spirit-led chairing made a difference. You will be offered templates, checklists, and practices to bring clarity and confidence to your work.

But even more than tools, my hope is that this book reminds you that your leadership is sacred. The way you chair a meeting, set an agenda, encourage dialogue, and pause for prayer is not merely functional—it is formational. It shapes the culture of the board and, in turn, the witness of the church. Every agenda item, every conversation, every prayer is part of a larger rhythm that either roots the body in God's call or distracts it from it.

You are not in this alone. You serve within a tradition of faithful leaders who, across centuries, have discerned together what God was asking of them. You are part of a body that is sustained by the Spirit's wisdom, not merely by human skill. And you are connected to other leaders through communities like the Effective Church Leadership Community (ECLC), where practices and resources are shared so that none of us needs to carry this role without support.

So as you turn these pages, I invite you to receive them as companions for the journey. Let them guide, but also let them reassure you. You will not chair perfectly. There will be moments of uncertainty, fatigue, and even frustration. But you can lead faithfully. You can create space for the Spirit to be heard. You can guide your board to stay rooted in calling, steady in discernment, and open to the new life God is growing among you.

Thank you for stepping into this sacred role. Thank you for being willing to serve as Mission Keeper, alongside the Vision Driver and the Mission Interpreter, so that together your congregation may remain rooted in its call and bear fruit for God's kingdom.

May this book serve as both encouragement and guide, reminding you that your leadership is not simply about managing but about keeping the church rooted in the Spirit's life-giving soil.

Part I
The Sacred Role of Chairperson

Planted by the Spirit, your leadership begins not in tasks but in calling. This section grounds you in the Spirit's placement and identity, inviting you to see chairpersonship as a sacred trust.

Planted by the Spirit

"But in fact God has placed the parts in the body, every one of them, just as he wanted them to be."

-1 Corinthians 12:18 (NIV)

Opening Reflection

Roots do not choose where they are planted. They reach downward into the soil that holds them, stretching toward streams of water, drawing life from the unseen depths. In the same way, your role as chairperson is not self-selected or randomly assigned—it is Spirit-given. Paul reminds us that God places each part of the body exactly where it is needed. You have been planted by the Spirit for this season, in this congregation, with these people.

Your leadership is a sacred trust. You are not here to manage tasks or maintain order alone. You are here to help the board listen for God's call, to anchor decisions in discernment, and to nurture the community's faithfulness. Like roots reaching for hidden streams, your leadership seeks nourishment in prayer, Scripture, and Spirit-led wisdom.

Suggested Practices

- Begin your day with prayer for the congregation's leaders.
- Before each meeting, pause for silence, inviting the Spirit to guide.
- Write down one way you see God at work in your board's life.
- Share words of gratitude with fellow leaders, planting encouragement.

Theological Framing

In *Embracing Our Call*, Chapter 1 reminds us that leadership begins with placement: "The Spirit has placed us here." Your role as chairperson is not about filling a slot but about embodying a sacred call. The **Calling–Energy–Resources–Discernment (CERD)** framework helps you see this role more clearly:

- **Calling**: You are entrusted with guiding the board to stay aligned with God's mission, asking always, "What is the Spirit inviting us toward?"

- **Energy**: Meetings can drain or inspire. Your leadership helps shape space where energy flows toward prayerful discernment rather than endless reports.
- **Resources**: Time, attention, and wisdom are resources to steward. You ensure they are used for mission, not maintenance alone.
- **Discernment**: At the center of it all, your task is to create room for Spirit-led listening, so that decisions reflect faith, not fear.

This redefines chairing from administration to spiritual stewardship. You are not merely an organizer; you are a cultivator of soil where discernment can grow.

Suggested Practices

- Frame every agenda with mission at the center.
- Encourage prayer pauses before significant votes.
- Ask CERD questions to re-ground discussions: "Does this reflect our calling? Where is our energy? What resources must we steward? What discernment is needed?"
- Remind the board regularly that its purpose is faithfulness, not efficiency.

Case Study and Practical Steps

A church governing body was considering whether to expand its outreach program. Some were concerned about the strain on finances; others feared volunteer burnout. The conversation quickly became tense, with members arguing about logistics rather than mission.

The chairperson chose to pause the discussion. They reminded the board of their calling and read 1 Corinthians 12:18. Then they invited silence, asking each member to consider how the Spirit might be placing them in this moment. After the pause, the conversation shifted. Members spoke less about scarcity and more about mission. They decided to begin with a smaller outreach initiative, using existing volunteers, while praying for how God might grow the effort in the future. The decision was not perfect, but it was Spirit-led, aligning with both mission and capacity.

First 48 Hours as Chair – A Checklist

1. **Pray Over Your Call**: Set aside time to thank God for entrusting you with this role.
2. **Meet with the Pastor**: Begin with prayer and conversation about hopes for the year.
3. **Review the Agenda Template**: Shape it so that discernment comes before routine business.
4. **Reach Out to the Board**: Send a short note of gratitude, naming your excitement to serve with them.
5. **Establish a Rhythm of Silence**: Decide how you will invite prayer pauses into your first meeting.

Suggested Practices

- Create space for testimony at your first meeting, allowing members to share where they see God at work.
- Begin building trust with one-on-one conversations with board members.
- Clarify roles and expectations early to prevent confusion.
- Commit to praying over each agenda item before your first meeting.

Closing

"You are planted where the Spirit wills."

You did not choose this soil, yet the Spirit has placed you here. Your leadership is not about control but about cultivation—helping the board root itself in God's calling, draw energy from prayerful rhythms, steward resources wisely, and act with discernment.

Discernment Prompts

- Where do you sense God's placement in your leadership today?
- What practices will help you remain rooted in calling rather than overwhelmed by tasks?
- How will you create space for discernment in your board's first gatherings?

Like a tree planted by streams of water, your leadership will flourish when rooted in the Spirit, bearing fruit that nourishes the body of Christ.

Roots of Leadership

"The whole body grows from him, as it is joined and held together by all the supporting ligaments. The body makes itself grow in that it builds itself up with love as each one does its part."

-Ephesians 4:16 (CEB)

Opening Reflection

Roots anchor a tree, drawing life from the soil and holding it steady through the seasons. Without roots, growth cannot endure. Leadership is much the same. As chairperson, your role is not simply about tasks or authority—it is about being rooted in God's Spirit, connected to the body of Christ, and drawing nourishment from calling, prayer, and discernment.

Paul's vision in Ephesians reminds us that the whole body grows only when each part does its work. Your leadership is one of those vital parts, joined with others, building up the church in love. Your roots matter, not only for your steadiness but also for the health of the entire body. When you are grounded in God's call, the board you lead is steadied, nourished, and able to flourish together.

Suggested Practices

- Reflect weekly on where your leadership feels rooted in God's Spirit.
- Begin each meeting by acknowledging the body's unity in Christ.
- Journal about what nourishes your leadership and what drains it.
- Pray for the strength to remain anchored when challenges arise.

Theological Framing

In *Embracing Our Call*, Chapter 2 reminds us that our identity as leaders flows from where we are planted. You are not defined by efficiency or authority but by faithfulness to the Spirit's placement. The **Calling–Energy–Resources–Discernment (CERD)** framework helps you see the deep roots of leadership:

- **Calling**: Your identity is shaped first by God's call, not by titles or roles. Leadership grows from listening for God's direction and guiding others toward mission.

- **Energy**: Roots carry energy throughout the body. As chair, you help channel life-giving energy into board conversations, ensuring that hope and prayer outweigh fear and fatigue.
- **Resources**: Just as roots absorb water and nutrients, your leadership draws on resources—Scripture, prayer, wisdom, and community—to nourish faithful decision-making.
- **Discernment**: Roots must know where to grow. Discernment directs your leadership, ensuring that choices emerge from Spirit-led reflection rather than impulse.

Your identity as chairperson is not separate from the body but deeply connected to it. The more deeply rooted you are in CERD, the more stable and fruitful your leadership will be.

Suggested Practices

- Revisit your sense of calling regularly, asking how God is shaping your role.
- Notice where board energy flows—encourage what sustains and redirect what depletes.
- Seek wisdom from Scripture and seasoned leaders as vital resources.
- Create space in meetings for silence, allowing discernment to deepen.

Case Study and Practical Steps

A church governing body struggled with conflict after their long-time treasurer stepped down. Anxiety about finances led meetings to spiral into heated debates. The board became reactive, focused more on defending positions than discerning God's call.

The chairperson sensed the board had lost its roots. At the next retreat, they invited members into reflection using Ephesians 4:16. Together, they asked: "How do we build one another up in love, even when tensions are high?" The chair guided the board through CERD:

- **Calling**: What is God asking us to remember about our mission in this moment?
- **Energy**: Where are we wasting energy in conflict, and where can we redirect it?
- **Resources**: What wisdom, financial guidance, and prayer can sustain us now?
- **Discernment**: What is the Spirit showing us about next faithful steps?

The exercise helped the board reframe their challenge. They decided to form a finance task group for clarity while refocusing meetings on mission. Tension did not vanish overnight, but unity grew as the board reclaimed its identity in love.

Leadership Identity Reflection

1. When do you feel most rooted in God's call as chairperson?
2. What practices nourish your leadership identity?
3. Where do you sense your leadership being drained, and how might you redirect that energy?
4. How does your leadership reflect connection to the whole body of Christ?

A downloadable version of this reflection guide is available through the Effective Church Leadership Community (ECLC).

Suggested Practices

- Schedule quarterly retreats to reflect on leadership identity as a board.
- Use the Leadership Identity Reflection personally each season.
- Encourage board members to name where they see one another's gifts in action.
- Model honesty by sharing how you stay rooted in calling during challenges.

Closing

"Your roots grow deep in God's call."

You are not a chairperson by chance. You are planted, rooted, and nourished by the Spirit for this season of leadership. By tending your roots through calling, energy, resources, and discernment, you strengthen not only yourself but the whole body of Christ.

Discernment Prompts

- How does your leadership identity reflect God's call today?
- What practices keep you rooted when storms arise?
- How can you help your board stay connected to the body's shared life in Christ?

May your leadership be like roots anchoring a tree—steady, nourished, and strong—drawing life from the Spirit and giving strength to the body you serve.

Part II
Leading with Discernment

Leadership flows not from control but from listening. In these chapters, you will discover how to shape agendas, foster dialogue, and cultivate practices of sacred listening that keep your board aligned with God's Spirit.

Shaping the Agenda

"Put God in charge of your work, then what you've planned will take place."

-Proverbs 16:3 (MSG)

Opening Reflection

An agenda is more than a list of topics. It is a riverbed, shaping how the current of conversation will flow. When the agenda is shallow, discussions meander or stagnate. When it is rigid, the Spirit has no space to move. But when crafted with prayerful intention, the agenda guides the board like a stream flowing toward God's call.

Proverbs reminds us to place our work under God's care. The agenda you prepare is not your own design alone—it is a framework for Spirit-led discernment. You are invited to craft it as an act of trust, surrendering the order of business to God's guidance. In doing so, the board moves beyond routine to participate in God's unfolding purpose.

Suggested Practices

- Review each agenda prayerfully before sending it out.
- Place discernment items at the top, before routine reports.
- Invite silence at key points to allow space for reflection.
- Begin each meeting by dedicating the agenda to God's care.

Theological Framing

In *Embracing Our Call*, Chapter 10 reminds us that agendas are not neutral—they reveal what we value. A Spirit-shaped agenda elevates calling above maintenance, discernment above routine. The **Calling–Energy–Resources–Discernment (CERD)** framework provides a lens for shaping agendas:

- **Calling**: Every agenda should help the board align with mission. Ask, "How does this meeting reflect our calling?"
- **Energy**: Energy flows toward what is prioritized. By placing prayer, discernment, and mission at the forefront, you channel energy into what matters most.
- **Resources**: Agendas steward time, one of your most valuable resources. Require that reports be submitted in writing at least three days before the meeting, so time together can focus on discernment and action.

- **Discernment**: An agenda that allows silence, prayer, and reflection creates conditions for listening to God.

Shaping the agenda is, therefore, a spiritual act. You are not simply organizing items—you are cultivating soil where discernment can grow and flourish.

Suggested Practices

- Ask CERD questions as you draft each agenda.
- Limit the number of action items to focus on what truly advances the mission.
- Require reports in writing at least three days in advance, and hold members accountable for preparation.
- Schedule time for prayerful pauses before major decisions.

Case Study and Practical Steps

A church governing body was considering whether to begin a new partnership with a local nonprofit. The agenda for the meeting was crowded—reports, budget updates, and announcements threatened to consume the time. The chairperson realized that if discernment was left to the end, the conversation would be rushed or neglected.

Instead, the chair shaped the agenda around calling. After opening prayer and silence, the board moved directly into a period of reflection: How does this partnership align with our mission? Members shared stories of how their church had served the community in the past and how this opportunity might extend that witness. Only after this extended discernment did the board move into reports and updates.

Because routine reports had been submitted in writing at least three days prior, members had time to review and reflect prayerfully before gathering. This freed the meeting for focused dialogue. Questions were asked, risks discussed, and hopes voiced. The decision that emerged was grounded not in haste but in Spirit-led discernment. The board left the meeting feeling that their time had been used faithfully, and their decision reflected God's purpose.

Spirit-Led Agenda Template

1. **Opening Prayer and Silence**
2. **Scripture Reflection or Devotional**
3. **Discernment Item(s)** – mission, calling, or key decisions
4. **Action Items** – requiring discussion or votes
5. **Routine Reports** – submitted in writing at least three days prior; acknowledged briefly unless action is required
6. **Closing Gratitude and Prayer**

A downloadable version of this template, with guiding questions, is available through the Effective Church Leadership Community (ECLC).

Suggested Practices

- Require reports in writing at least three days before the meeting, giving members time to read and pray.
- Acknowledge reports briefly in meetings, lifting only items that need action.
- End meetings with gratitude, naming one way the Spirit was present.
- Review and revise the agenda format annually with the board.

Closing

"An agenda shaped by the Spirit flows toward God's call."

As chairperson, you are invited to see the agenda not as paperwork but as a prayer. When you place discernment at the center, ensure reports arrive in time for preparation, and entrust the flow of the meeting to God, the board becomes a channel for the Spirit's work.

Discernment Prompts

- How does your agenda reflect God's purpose rather than efficiency alone?
- Where might routine reports be trimmed to create space for discernment?
- What practices can help your board trust the Spirit to shape the flow of meetings?

Like streams guided by a riverbed, your agendas can direct energy, attention, and prayer toward God's call—helping the board flow faithfully into the mission prepared for them.

Listening for the Spirit

"The LORD said, 'Go out and stand on the mountain in front of me.' The LORD was passing by. A very strong wind tore through the mountains and broke apart the rocks in front of the LORD. But the LORD wasn't in the wind. After the wind, there was an earthquake. But the LORD wasn't in the earthquake. After the earthquake, there was a fire. But the LORD wasn't in the fire. After the fire, there was a gentle whisper."

-1 Kings 19:11–12 (CEV)

Opening Reflection

Winds roar, earthquakes shake, fires blaze. Yet the prophet discovered that God's presence was not in the noise, but in the gentle whisper. The Spirit speaks in ways that the world often overlooks—through silence, stillness, and quiet attentiveness.

As chairperson, you are called to foster this posture of listening within the board. In meetings, voices can rise quickly with opinions, numbers, or anxieties. But faithful leadership requires the space to pause, breathe, and listen for the Spirit's whisper. Just as soil cradles seeds before growth is visible, silence and listening hold space for God's direction before decisions are made.

Listening is not passive. It is an act of faith. When you create rhythms of listening, you remind the board that discernment does not come from argument alone, but from the Spirit's gentle, guiding presence.

Suggested Practices

- Begin meetings with extended silence, inviting members to listen for God's whisper.
- Use Scripture not just as inspiration but as a grounding for listening.
- Encourage pauses after discussion to reflect before voting.
- Remind the board that listening is as important as speaking.

Theological Framing

In *Sacred Listening*, Chapter 1, we are reminded that listening is at the heart of discernment. True leadership is not about rushing to solutions but creating space for the Spirit to speak. Your role as chair is to help cultivate this space—shaping meetings not as debates but as conversations undergirded by prayer.

The **Calling–Energy–Resources–Discernment (CERD)** framework deepens this practice:

- **Calling**: Listening reconnects the board to God's call. Rather than reacting to pressures, pausing to listen reminds everyone of mission.
- **Energy**: Meetings without pauses drain energy. Listening restores it, giving strength for faithful work.
- **Resources**: Time is a precious resource. By dedicating time to silence and listening, you steward it toward God's purposes rather than rushing decisions.
- **Discernment**: Listening is the very heart of discernment. Without it, decisions are human-driven; with it, they become Spirit-led.

When you shape meetings around listening, you guide the board into a deeper rhythm—one where silence becomes fertile soil for God's word to grow.

Suggested Practices

- Schedule silence into the agenda as a standing practice.
- Frame discussions with guiding questions rather than debates.
- Invite the board to reflect on where they hear God's call before making decisions.
- Encourage journaling between meetings as a way of listening to the Spirit.

Case Study and Practical Steps

A church governing body was considering whether to close one of its long-running ministries. The financial strain was significant, but the ministry still carried deep meaning for many members. The board was divided, and conversations quickly became heated.

Sensing the rising tension, the chairperson paused the discussion. They invited the board into five minutes of silence, reading aloud 1 Kings 19:11–12. At first the silence felt awkward, but gradually members began to settle. Afterward, the chair asked each person to share what they sensed during the quiet. The tone shifted. Instead of arguments, people spoke of grief, hope, and faith.

Through this practice, the board discerned to close the ministry with care while creating new opportunities for service that aligned more fully with the church's mission. The decision was not easy, but because it was grounded in listening, it carried a sense of peace and unity.

Sacred Listening Practice – The Mini-Examine

1. Pause in silence. Breathe deeply and become aware of God's presence.
2. Ask: Where did I notice God's presence in our work today?
3. Ask: Where did I resist God's leading?
4. Offer gratitude and a prayer for wisdom in the next step.

A downloadable version of this practice is available through the Effective Church Leadership Community (ECLC).

Suggested Practices

- Use the Mini-Examine at the end of each meeting to reflect together.
- Begin major decisions with Scripture and silence before discussion.
- Encourage leaders to practice personal silence daily as part of their own rule of life.
- Host an annual retreat focused solely on listening for the Spirit.

Closing

"In silence, the Spirit speaks."

As chairperson, you are entrusted with more than guiding conversation—you are called to guide the board into listening. In silence, the Spirit whispers wisdom; in listening, the body discovers its path.

Discernment Prompts

- Where do you hear the Spirit's whisper in your board's work?
- How might silence become a more regular practice in your leadership?
- What rhythms of listening could help your board root decisions more deeply in God's call?

Like streams whispering truth and soil cradling seeds, your leadership nurtures the conditions where God's quiet voice can be heard and trusted.

Facilitating Dialogue

"For where two or three gather together because they are mine, I will be right there among them."

-Matthew 18:20 (TLB)

Opening Reflection

Streams that flow alone may be strong, but when they merge, they create a river of greater depth and power. Dialogue in leadership is like those streams—individual voices coming together, not to erase differences, but to create harmony in shared movement. As chairperson, your sacred task is to help the board merge its voices in ways that honor both diversity and unity, guiding the flow toward God's call.

Jesus assures us that wherever two or three gather in his name, his presence is there. Dialogue, then, is not simply human exchange—it is a Spirit-filled practice. In the midst of board meetings, where conflict and differing opinions naturally arise, you are called to make space for this holy presence. True dialogue is not about winning an argument but about weaving the board together in love, humility, and discernment.

Suggested Practices

- Begin dialogue by reminding the board of Christ's presence in your gathering.
- Encourage open-hearted sharing rather than quick rebuttals.
- Use silence between responses to slow the pace and deepen listening.
- Pray at moments of tension, inviting the Spirit to guide words and hearts.

Theological Framing

In *Embracing Our Call*, Chapter 23 underscores that unity is not uniformity. The board's strength lies in its ability to hold diverse voices while remaining anchored in calling. Dialogue is the practice that makes this possible. It transforms meetings from debates into spaces of discernment, where differences are not erased but placed in the service of God's mission.

The **Calling–Energy–Resources–Discernment (CERD)** framework shows how dialogue nurtures leadership:

- **Calling**: Dialogue helps clarify the congregation's mission. By listening deeply, the board hears not only each other but the Spirit's call.
- **Energy**: Healthy dialogue channels energy into collaboration rather than conflict. It strengthens trust and renews passion for ministry.
- **Resources**: Time, patience, and words are resources to steward. Spirit-led dialogue values these, ensuring that conversations are fruitful rather than draining.
- **Discernment**: Dialogue is the soil where discernment grows. When every voice is heard with respect, the Spirit's guidance becomes clearer.

Your leadership as chair is not to dominate conversation but to shape it—helping the board remember that dialogue is itself a form of prayer.

Suggested Practices

- Establish covenantal ground rules for dialogue rooted in love and respect.
- Use CERD questions to frame conversations that risk becoming polarized.
- Encourage members to name where they see God in the dialogue.
- Redirect unhelpful conflict back to calling, ensuring focus on mission.

Case Study and Practical Steps

A church governing body was considering whether to expand worship services to include a new evening gathering. Some believed this would reach new people; others feared it would overextend volunteers. The discussion quickly became heated, with frustration surfacing in raised voices.

The chairperson paused the conversation. They reminded the board of Jesus' promise in Matthew 18:20, that Christ is present whenever the body gathers. They then invited a prayer of silence and guided the group through structured dialogue. Each member was asked to share their perspective without interruption, followed by others repeating back what they heard before responding. The tone shifted. What began as conflict became a deeper conversation about calling and capacity.

Through this dialogue, the board discerned that while an evening service was not sustainable in the immediate season, they could pilot a quarterly evening worship as a step toward outreach. The decision emerged not from division but from shared listening and prayer.

Dialogue Facilitation Guide

1. **Ground the Conversation**: Begin with prayer and Scripture.
2. **Establish Space**: Invite each member to share without interruption.
3. **Reflect Back**: Encourage participants to repeat what they heard before responding.
4. **Name Calling**: Ask how each perspective connects to mission.
5. **Discern Next Steps**: Identify areas of agreement and where prayer is still needed.

A downloadable version of this guide, with facilitation prompts, is available through the Effective Church Leadership Community (ECLC).

Suggested Practices

- Use the Dialogue Facilitation Guide when navigating contentious issues.
- Train board members in active listening, modeling patience and humility.
- Close difficult conversations with gratitude, naming what was learned.
- Encourage testimony, letting members share stories rather than only opinions.

Closing

"In dialogue, the Spirit weaves unity."

Your role as chairperson is to ensure that dialogue is not reduced to debate. When you create space for respectful listening, prayerful silence, and Spirit-centered sharing, you help the board become more than a collection of voices—you help it become the body of Christ discerning together.

Discernment Prompts

- How does your facilitation invite the Spirit's presence into dialogue?
- Where might your board need to move from debate into deeper listening?
- How can you remind members that dialogue itself is a form of prayer?

Like streams merging in harmony, Spirit-led dialogue flows into unity, carrying the board toward decisions that reflect God's call and strengthen the body's witness.

Part III
Anchoring in Mission

The roots of leadership sink deep into mission. This section explores how to align policies with practice, guide the board through the seasons of the year, and nurture the whole body so that every decision reflects God's call.

Policy to Practice

"The LORD hates false scales, but delights in accurate weights."

-Proverbs 11:1 (CEB)

Opening Reflection

Scales that are unbalanced mislead and harm, but those that are true bring fairness and trust. Policies in the life of the church are much like those scales. When faithfully aligned with mission, they ensure balance, integrity, and health. When ignored or misapplied, they distort the body's witness and weaken its roots.

As chairperson, you are entrusted with helping the board ensure that policies are not words on paper but living guides for practice. Policies are not meant to burden the church with bureaucracy; they are frameworks that shape faithfulness. Just as soil sustains roots so that trees may flourish, Spirit-led policies sustain the ministry of the church, grounding decisions in justice, transparency, and mission.

Your task is to help the board translate policy into practice—to ask how guidelines and structures nurture discipleship, protect resources, and reflect God's call. In doing so, you ensure that the body remains steady and trustworthy, a tree bearing fruit season after season.

Suggested Practices

- Review policies prayerfully, asking how they reflect mission.
- Connect every policy discussion to calling and discernment.
- Regularly ask, "How does this policy translate into practice?"
- Celebrate moments when faithful policies protect or advance ministry.

Theological Framing

In *Embracing Our Call*, Chapter 9 reminds us that policies are not constraints but tools for stewardship. They provide the clarity needed to sustain ministry and prevent harm. When guided by prayer, they become trellises on which healthy practices grow.

The **Calling–Energy–Resources–Discernment (CERD)** framework offers a way to ground policy in Spirit-led leadership:

- **Calling**: Policies should always serve the mission. If a policy distracts from or contradicts calling, it must be reexamined.
- **Energy**: Policies can either drain or sustain energy. Spirit-led policies reduce confusion and conflict, freeing energy for ministry.
- **Resources**: Policies steward resources—finances, buildings, people—with integrity. They ensure accountability and fairness in the body.
- **Discernment**: Policies require ongoing reflection. A faithful board asks, "Does this policy still serve God's purpose in this season?"

Your leadership ensures that policies are not static documents but living commitments, revised and practiced with prayer, aligning the church with God's enduring mission.

Suggested Practices

- Establish an annual rhythm for policy review, guided by CERD.
- Encourage the board to pray before adopting or revising policies.
- Frame every policy decision in terms of calling, not just compliance.
- In times of conflict, return to policies as shared agreements that reflect mission.

Case Study and Practical Steps

A church governing body faced conflict when questions arose about building use. Community groups requested access, but there were no clear guidelines. Some board members worried about liability, while others stressed the church's call to hospitality. Without policy, every request became a debate, draining time and energy.

The chairperson guided the board into a season of prayerful discernment. They asked: "How does building use connect with our calling? What energy is drained without clear guidelines? How can resources be stewarded faithfully?" Using CERD, the board developed a building use policy that reflected both mission and wisdom.

The policy affirmed hospitality while ensuring safety and accountability. Groups were welcomed with clear expectations, and the church's staff had clarity on procedures. What once caused conflict became an expression of calling. The chair later reflected, "The policy did more than solve a problem. It gave us a way to live out our mission with consistency."

Policy Alignment Checklist

1. Does this policy clearly reflect the church's mission and calling?
2. Does it sustain energy by reducing confusion and conflict?
3. Does it steward financial, physical, and human resources with integrity?
4. Does it invite ongoing discernment, allowing for revision as seasons change?
5. Is it written and communicated in a way that encourages faithful practice?

A downloadable version of this checklist, with facilitation questions, is available through the Effective Church Leadership Community (ECLC).

Suggested Practices

- Use the Policy Alignment Checklist whenever adopting or revising policies.
- Involve ministry leaders and the congregation in policy review where appropriate.
- Share stories of how policies have strengthened the church's witness.
- Train new leaders in how policies shape faithful practice.

Closing

"Policies rooted in the Spirit bear faithful fruit."

Policies are not the heart of the church, but they protect and nurture the heart's rhythms. As chairperson, your leadership ensures that policies are not forgotten or misused but are faithfully translated into practices that embody God's call.

Discernment Prompts

- How do your current policies reflect God's mission?
- Where might policies need to be refreshed to better align with calling?
- How can you help the board see policies not as burdens but as guides for faithfulness?

May your leadership be like streams nourishing roots and soil sustaining growth—ensuring that the church's structures support life, fruit, and faithfulness in every season.

Rhythm of the Year

"There is a time for everything, and a season for every activity under the heavens."

-Ecclesiastes 3:1 (NIV)

Opening Reflection

The seasons turn without our control. Leaves fall, snow rests, blossoms return, and fruit ripens in its time. Streams flow steadily, rising and receding with rains. In this rhythm, creation testifies that life is not random but ordered, woven with times of planting, waiting, harvesting, and resting.

So it is with the life of the church. As chairperson, you are entrusted with helping the board recognize and embrace the rhythm of the year. Leadership cannot be lived only in urgent decisions or reactive measures. It flourishes when guided by seasons—times for listening, times for planning, times for action, and times for rest.

When the board's work follows the Spirit's rhythm, it avoids exhaustion and finds deeper clarity. Like trees rooted through the changing year, your leadership can hold steady, trusting that every season has its purpose under heaven.

Suggested Practices

- Begin each new quarter with a prayer of dedication for the season ahead.
- Reflect on the church year (Advent, Lent, Pentecost) as a guide for rhythms of discernment.
- Plan seasonal pauses for reflection and evaluation.
- Name aloud which season the board is in: planting, tending, harvesting, or resting.

Theological Framing

In *Sacred Listening*, Chapter 6 highlights that discernment is sustained through rhythms, not random bursts. A healthy board does not wait for crises to listen for God but practices listening across the year. These rhythms anchor leadership in calling and prevent burnout.

The **Calling–Energy–Resources–Discernment (CERD)** framework provides a way to shape an annual rhythm:

- **Calling**: Each season asks, "What is God calling us to focus on now?" In some seasons it may be vision, in others, stewardship or care.
- **Energy**: Energy is finite. By honoring rhythms, you help the board pace its work, renewing energy in times of rest and channeling it in seasons of action.
- **Resources**: Resources must be reviewed regularly. Aligning budgets, staff, and ministries with the rhythm of the year ensures resources serve mission faithfully.
- **Discernment**: Rhythms create space for ongoing discernment. Rather than asking only in crisis, the board learns to listen consistently, trusting the Spirit in every season.

By guiding the board into annual patterns, you remind them that leadership is not about urgency but about faithfulness across time.

Suggested Practices

- Create an annual cycle for budget planning, ministry review, and visioning.
- Align board retreats with seasons of discernment (e.g., Advent or Lent).
- Encourage the board to see each meeting as part of a larger rhythm, not an isolated event.
- Use CERD questions each season to guide reflection.

Case Study and Practical Steps

A church governing body was struggling with exhaustion. Meetings often ran long, and decisions felt rushed. Members admitted they were reacting to issues rather than shaping the life of the congregation with purpose. The chairperson recognized that the board had no rhythm—it was functioning in constant urgency.

At the next retreat, the chair introduced Ecclesiastes 3:1 and asked, "What season are we in right now?" The group reflected on calling, energy, resources, and discernment. They realized that instead of trying to do everything at once, they needed an annual rhythm.

Together they shaped a simple *Annual Discernment Calendar*.

- **Winter**: Visioning and prayer, grounding the year in calling.
- **Spring**: Planning and preparing ministries, aligning resources.
- **Summer**: Rest, renewal, and mid-year reflection.
- **Fall**: Stewardship and harvest, celebrating ministries and preparing budgets.

This rhythm changed their work. Meetings became more focused, energy more balanced, and decisions more connected to calling. The congregation noticed, too—leaders were less frantic and more prayerful. What once felt overwhelming began to feel sustainable and Spirit-led.

Annual Discernment Calendar

1. **Quarterly Reflection**: Dedicate one meeting each season to prayer, reflection, and evaluation.
2. **Seasonal Themes**: Identify focus areas—vision, planning, rest, stewardship.
3. **Mission Connection**: Ask how the church's calling is expressed in this season.
4. **Discernment Pause**: Build in silence before major decisions each quarter.
5. **Celebration**: At least once a year, dedicate a meeting to gratitude and testimony.

A downloadable version of this calendar, with facilitation prompts, is available through the Effective Church Leadership Community (ECLC).

Suggested Practices

- Post the Annual Discernment Calendar where the board can see it throughout the year.
- Involve ministry leaders in seasonal reflections, broadening the circle of discernment.
- Hold at least one congregational forum annually to share the board's reflections.
- Use the rhythm to anticipate workload, preventing burnout by spreading work evenly.

Closing

"In the rhythm of the year, the Spirit guides each season."

Your leadership as chairperson is about more than running meetings—it is about guiding the board into holy time. By shaping an annual rhythm, you help the church root itself in God's steady flow. Seasons of planting, tending, resting, and harvesting each carry purpose, each guided by the Spirit's hand.

Discernment Prompts

- How does your board's current rhythm align with God's timing?
- Which season do you sense your board is in right now—planting, tending, harvesting, or resting?
- How might an annual rhythm create sustainability and faithfulness in your leadership?

Like seasons turning and streams flowing through time, your leadership can help the board walk not in frenzy but in faith, trusting that God has appointed a time for every purpose under heaven.

Nurturing the Whole Body

"If one part of the body hurts, we hurt all over. If one part of the body is honored, the whole body will be happy."

-1 Corinthians 12:26 (CEV)

Opening Reflection

The body of Christ is not a collection of scattered pieces—it is a living, breathing whole. Roots intertwine beneath the soil, unseen yet essential, strengthening one another against storms. Streams nourish not just a single branch but the entire grove, sustaining life for all. So it is with the church: when one part suffers, all suffer; when one part flourishes, all rejoice.

As chairperson, you are called to help nurture this wholeness. Your leadership is not only about guiding the board but also about fostering harmony between board, pastor, and congregation. When each part is honored, connected, and aligned with God's mission, the whole body thrives. Your task is to ensure that leadership does not become fragmented but remains rooted together in love.

Suggested Practices

- Begin meetings with prayers for both the congregation and pastor.
- Regularly remind the board that decisions affect the whole body, not just the boardroom.
- Celebrate ministries that demonstrate unity and shared purpose.
- Encourage testimonies of both joy and struggle, holding them together in prayer.

Theological Framing

In *Embracing Our Call*, Chapter 24 highlights that governance exists to serve the whole body, not to isolate a few leaders. Leadership is healthiest when it nurtures connections across every part of the church.

The **Calling–Energy–Resources–Discernment (CERD)** framework helps shape this vision:

- **Calling**: The church's mission belongs to the entire body. The board discerns direction not for itself but for the congregation as a whole.
- **Energy**: Collaboration renews energy. When board, pastor, and congregation share responsibility, energy multiplies rather than drains.
- **Resources**: Resources are gifts entrusted to the whole body. Decisions about money, time, or space should honor the needs of all.
- **Discernment**: Listening is communal. Spirit-led discernment requires engaging the voices of pastor, board, and congregation in dialogue.

Your leadership nurtures unity by ensuring that no part of the body is ignored. Instead, the entire church becomes a woven whole, strengthened by connection and alignment with God's mission.

Suggested Practices

- Use CERD questions to test whether board decisions reflect the needs of the whole body.
- Include the pastor's voice early in discussions to foster alignment.
- Encourage congregational input through listening circles or surveys.
- Remind the board often: "We serve the whole, not ourselves."

Case Study and Practical Steps

A church governing body faced conflict over how to allocate its budget. Some leaders wanted to invest more in community outreach, while others stressed facility repairs. The pastor felt torn between both priorities, and the congregation grew restless as rumors spread about disagreement.

The chairperson recognized that the board was treating the decision as a zero-sum conflict rather than a communal discernment. At the next meeting, the chair invited members to reflect on 1 Corinthians 12:26: "If one part of the body hurts, we hurt all over. If one part of the body is honored, the whole body will be happy."

They then used a *Collaboration Map* to visualize alignment. The board noted how outreach expressed the church's calling, how facilities sustained energy for ministry, and how both required resources. By inviting the pastor and congregational leaders into the discussion, the board reframed the decision. Ultimately, they chose a balanced approach: immediate repairs for safety while launching a new outreach pilot.

The process not only resolved the budget question but also strengthened trust. The congregation felt heard, the pastor felt supported, and the board discovered that nurturing the whole body was less about compromise and more about shared mission.

Collaboration Map

1. Write the church's mission statement in the center.
2. List current board decisions and how they connect to calling.
3. Record the pastor's initiatives and where they align with mission.
4. Gather congregational input through stories or surveys.
5. Draw arrows between areas of alignment and identify gaps.

A downloadable version of this tool, with facilitation prompts, is available through the Effective Church Leadership Community (ECLC).

Sidebar: Chair–Pastor Partnership

Your relationship with the pastor is one of the most vital ways to nurture the whole body. A healthy partnership provides stability, clarity, and trust for the congregation. Meet regularly to pray, share observations, and align visions. Discuss challenges honestly, but present a united spirit before the board. When the chair and pastor walk together in trust, the church feels it, and the whole body flourishes.

Suggested Practices

- Schedule monthly meetings with the pastor for prayer and alignment.
- Review the Collaboration Map quarterly with board and pastor together.
- Invite congregational testimonies at least once a year to celebrate unity.
- Publicly affirm the partnership between chair and pastor as a model of shared leadership.

Closing

"In nurturing the body, the Spirit binds us as one."

As chairperson, your calling is not to lead in isolation but to weave together the strands of board, pastor, and congregation into a unified whole. By fostering collaboration, honoring each part, and guiding all toward calling, you help the body live as Christ intends—suffering together, rejoicing together, and growing together.

Discernment Prompts

- How does your leadership foster unity across board, pastor, and congregation?
- Where do you see gaps in energy or collaboration that need attention?
- How can you strengthen the chair–pastor partnership to nurture the whole body?

Like roots intertwining for strength and streams sustaining life, your leadership nourishes the church so that it may flourish as one body in Christ.

Part IV
Remaining Rooted

Enduring leadership requires steady rhythms. These closing chapters invite you to cultivate a rule of life, foster communal practices that prevent burnout, and guide the board toward a future firmly rooted in God's mission.

Part IV
Renaming Rounced

Crisis and Change

"There's more to come: We continue to shout our praise even when we're hemmed in with troubles, because we know how troubles can develop passionate patience in us, and how that patience in turn forges the tempered steel of virtue, keeping us alert for whatever God will do next. In alert expectancy such as this, we're never left feeling shortchanged. Quite the contrary—we can't round up enough containers to hold everything God generously pours into our lives through the Holy Spirit!"

-Romans 5:3–5 (MSG)

Opening Reflection

Storms bend branches, yet roots grow deeper in the rain. Crisis can feel like destruction—like winds too strong for your leadership to withstand, or soil washed away before it can hold. But the witness of faith reminds us that storms, while unsettling, can also renew. They strip away what is fragile, strengthen what is steady, and enrich the soil for new growth.

As chairperson, you will lead through seasons of crisis and change. Whether financial shortfalls, pastoral transitions, or community struggles, your task is not to remove all pain but to help the board discover meaning and direction within it. Romans reminds us that trouble develops patience, patience shapes character, and character births hope. In crisis, your leadership helps the board move from fear to resilience, from reaction to Spirit-led perseverance.

Suggested Practices

- Begin every crisis conversation with prayer and silence, grounding the body in God's presence.
- Speak truthfully about the challenge while naming hope.
- Remind the board of God's past faithfulness as an anchor for the present.
- Close crisis discussions with gratitude, no matter how small.

Theological Framing

In *Embracing Our Call*, Chapter 25 teaches that crisis is not an interruption of leadership but a part of it. Change and disruption reveal what is essential and test whether the board will choose fear or faith.

The **Calling–Energy–Resources–Discernment (CERD)** framework provides direction for Spirit-led crisis leadership:

- **Calling**: Crisis can obscure calling. The temptation is to focus only on survival. Your role is to ask, "What deeper call is God revealing in this moment?"

- **Energy**: Crises drain energy quickly. By pausing, praying, and celebrating small victories, you redirect energy from panic to perseverance.
- **Resources**: Crises expose vulnerabilities in finances, facilities, and leadership. Faithful stewardship means facing limits honestly, while trusting that God provides enough for the next step.
- **Discernment**: In crisis, urgency presses hard. Yet discernment requires stillness. Leading the board to wait on the Spirit—even briefly—prevents rash choices and opens space for clarity.

Your leadership is not about controlling storms but about steadying the body while roots grow deeper.

Suggested Practices

- Reframe crisis conversations around CERD questions.
- Invite testimonies of God's faithfulness in past struggles to renew courage.
- Establish a rhythm of shorter, prayer-filled meetings during long seasons of change.
- Use Scripture as a grounding anchor, reading aloud before key decisions.

Case Study and Practical Steps

A church governing body faced turmoil when their pastor announced an unexpected departure. The congregation felt abandoned, and the board was torn between rushing to hire a replacement or pausing for discernment. Anxiety ran high, and meetings began to fracture.

The chairperson recognized that the board needed to slow down. At the next gathering, they read Romans 5:3–5 and invited five minutes of silence. Afterward, each member was asked to reflect on where they sensed God's presence in the midst of change. The conversation shifted. Rather than debating candidates, the board began to ask deeper questions: "What is God teaching us in this season? How can we listen before we act?"

Together, they created a plan. They would call an interim pastor to guide worship and care, while the board and congregation entered a season of listening and prayer. By resisting urgency and embracing discernment, the church not only weathered the transition but emerged with renewed clarity about its mission.

Crisis Discernment Toolkit

1. **Pause for Prayer**: Begin every crisis conversation with silence and Scripture.
2. **Name the Reality**: Acknowledge challenges truthfully, without blame or denial.
3. **Ask CERD Questions**: Where is God's call? Where is energy drained or renewed? How must we steward resources? What discernment is needed?
4. **Communicate Transparently**: Keep the congregation informed with honesty and hope.
5. **Discern the Next Faithful Step**: Focus not on solving everything but on one Spirit-led action at a time.

A downloadable version of this toolkit, with facilitation questions, is available through the Effective Church Leadership Community (ECLC).

Suggested Practices

- Gather the congregation for prayer during seasons of crisis, not just the board.
- Encourage leaders to journal how God is speaking in moments of change.
- Use a visible sign of hope—a candle, a cross, or Scripture—as a reminder in meetings.
- Return regularly to the Crisis Discernment Toolkit until stability is regained.

Closing

"In crisis, the Spirit forges deeper roots."

As chairperson, your leadership is tested most in times of upheaval. Yet crisis can become the soil where perseverance, character, and hope grow. By grounding decisions in calling, stewarding resources faithfully, and leading the board into prayerful discernment, you help the body move not only through crisis but also toward deeper trust in God.

Discernment Prompts

- How does this crisis invite deeper discernment rather than quick fixes?
- Where might God be strengthening the roots of your congregation through this change?
- What practices of resilience can help your board trust the Spirit's guidance in uncertainty?

Like soil renewed after rain and branches strengthened by storms, your leadership in crisis can help the church not only endure but grow, rooted more deeply in God's enduring call.

Succession

"You have often heard me teach. Now I want you to tell these same things to followers who can be trusted to tell others."

-2 Timothy 2:2 (CEV)

Opening Reflection

Seeds are planted not for today alone but for the harvest to come. A stream does not keep water for itself but carries life forward to fields downstream. So it is with leadership in the church. Your time as chairperson is a season—a sacred opportunity to guide, nurture, and plant. Yet your calling is also to prepare others, ensuring that the mission continues with strength after your service concludes.

Paul's words to Timothy remind us that teaching, wisdom, and calling are never meant to stop with one generation of leaders. They are entrusted and passed on, multiplied through those who come after. Succession, then, is not an afterthought but a sacred practice of stewardship. You are invited to plant seeds of leadership now so that when your season ends, others will be ready to carry the call forward.

Suggested Practices

- Pray regularly for God to raise up new leaders in your congregation.
- Invite potential leaders to shadow you in board responsibilities.
- Share openly about both the joys and challenges of leadership.
- Remember: succession is about continuity of mission, not replacing yourself.

Theological Framing

In *Embracing Our Call*, Chapter 10 reminds us that leadership is always temporary and entrusted for a season. Healthy boards understand that no one serves forever, and preparing for transitions is as important as leading in the present. Succession is not about filling an empty seat—it is about stewarding the leadership of the church with care and foresight.

The **Calling–Energy–Resources–Discernment (CERD)** framework illuminates succession as Spirit-led stewardship:

- **Calling**: Succession ensures that leadership continues to reflect the church's mission, not just the style or gifts of one leader. Passing on the call is the heart of succession.
- **Energy**: New leaders bring fresh vitality. Intentional mentoring helps energy flow into the body without disruption when transitions occur.
- **Resources**: Leadership itself is a resource to be stewarded. Succession ensures wisdom is not lost but handed down to those ready to serve.
- **Discernment**: Choosing future leaders is not merely about skill but about prayerful listening. Discernment asks, "Who is God raising up for this next season?"

Your role as chairperson includes guiding the board to see succession not with anxiety but with hope. Seeds planted today will grow into leadership tomorrow, if watered with prayer and tended with care.

Suggested Practices

- Encourage the board to view leadership as a trust that is always shared and temporary.
- Use CERD in mentoring: show how calling, energy, resources, and discernment shape leadership decisions.
- Invite conversations about leadership development during calm seasons, not only during transitions.
- Affirm emerging leaders publicly, recognizing their gifts as signs of God's provision.

Case Study and Practical Steps

A church governing body realized that many of its leaders were nearing the end of their terms. Anxiety grew as members asked, "Who will lead after us?" The temptation was to wait until the last minute and scramble for names.

The chairperson took a different approach. They prayed intentionally for God to reveal new leaders and invited two younger members to shadow them in their role. These individuals were given space to observe agenda preparation, help facilitate portions of meetings, and join conversations with the pastor. The chair also met with them privately for reflection, asking, "What do you sense God might be calling you to in leadership?"

By the time elections came, the board had clear candidates who were not only willing but prepared. The transition was smooth, and the congregation celebrated the continuity of leadership. The chair reflected: "Succession was not about me leaving—it was about planting seeds of trust and discernment so that leadership could flourish beyond me."

Succession Planning Guide

1. **Pray and Identify**: Ask God to reveal individuals with gifts for leadership.
2. **Invite and Include**: Encourage potential leaders to shadow or participate in small responsibilities.
3. **Mentor and Reflect**: Share experiences honestly, highlighting both strengths and struggles.
4. **Discern Together**: In prayer, ask who God is raising up for the next season.
5. **Prepare and Release**: Create space for new leaders to lead before formal transitions.

A downloadable version of this guide, with reflection questions and mentoring prompts, is available through the Effective Church Leadership Community (ECLC).

Suggested Practices

- Pair current leaders with emerging leaders for mentorship.
- Celebrate leadership transitions as signs of God's faithfulness.
- Keep a record of lessons learned during your chairmanship to pass along.

- Meet with the pastor to discern together who might be prepared for future leadership.

Closing

"In succession, the Spirit plants seeds for tomorrow."

Your leadership is not complete until you have nurtured others to lead after you. Succession is part of your sacred trust as chairperson—entrusting wisdom, nurturing gifts, and ensuring that calling continues unbroken.

Discernment Prompts

- How are you preparing others to carry the call beyond your season of leadership?
- Who in your congregation might God be raising up for the next chapter?
- What practices can you put in place to ensure smooth, Spirit-led transitions?

Like seeds planted for future harvest and streams carrying life downstream, your leadership in succession ensures that the Spirit's work will continue to flow long after your season is done.

Rule of Life

"They are like trees along a riverbank bearing luscious fruit each season without fail. Their leaves shall never wither, and all they do shall prosper."

-Psalm 1:3 (TLB)

Opening Reflection

A tree planted by flowing water does not strain to bear fruit—it simply abides, season after season, in the rhythm of nourishment and rest. Its leaves remain green, not because it avoids dry winds or scorching heat, but because its roots reach deeply into soil saturated by streams.

So it is with leadership. As chairperson, you are often pulled by the demands of meetings, agendas, crises, and expectations. Without steady rhythms, the work can exhaust you. But when your life is shaped by a *rule of life*—a pattern of practices that root you in God's presence—your leadership is sustained. The Spirit provides fruit not just for a season, but for the long journey ahead.

A rule of life is not a rigid schedule but a rhythm that nurtures body, mind, and spirit. It steadies your leadership and prevents burnout, reminding you that faithfulness is not found in endless activity but in rootedness in God.

Suggested Practices

- Begin and end each day with a moment of prayerful stillness.
- Keep Sabbath as a sacred rhythm, protecting it from the press of tasks.
- Establish a weekly time to reflect on where you sensed God's presence.
- Share your rule of life with a trusted friend for encouragement and accountability.

Theological Framing

In *Sacred Listening*, Chapter 6, the importance of rhythm is emphasized: discernment is not sustained by intensity alone but by steady practices that keep leaders rooted. Without intentional rhythms, boards and leaders alike can lose focus, energy, and hope.

The **Calling–Energy–Resources–Discernment (CERD)** framework offers a way to understand a rule of life as spiritual leadership discipline:

- **Calling**: A rule of life helps you return, again and again, to your true calling. It keeps you centered in God's mission rather than in tasks or titles.
- **Energy**: Leadership demands energy. A rule of life replenishes rather than depletes, ensuring you can serve with strength and joy.
- **Resources**: Your time, body, and spirit are resources God has entrusted to you. A rule of life is how you steward these gifts faithfully.
- **Discernment**: A rule of life slows you down, creating space to listen. It transforms leadership from reactive decision-making into Spirit-led discernment.

As chairperson, you are also invited to guide the board into shared rhythms. A communal rule of life—praying before meetings, pausing for silence, reviewing mission regularly—keeps the body aligned with God's steady flow.

Suggested Practices

- Develop a personal rule of life in conversation with your spiritual director or mentor.
- Invite your board to reflect on shared practices that sustain discernment.
- Revisit your rule of life quarterly, adjusting for new seasons.
- Encourage practices of rest and prayer in both personal and communal leadership.

Case Study and Practical Steps

A church governing body had grown weary. Meetings stretched long, energy was thin, and members confessed they were running on empty. The chairperson realized that while the board was diligent in tasks, it lacked sustaining rhythms. They invited the board to create a simple rule of life together.

The process began with reflection: "Where do you sense God in your week? What practices renew you?" Members named prayer walks, quiet mornings, and shared meals. Together they agreed to three rhythms: opening each meeting with extended silence, dedicating one meeting each quarter to mission reflection, and ending every meeting with gratitude.

The change was gradual but noticeable. The silence grounded them. The quarterly reflections re-centered calling. Gratitude lifted weariness. Members began carrying these practices into their own lives. What once felt like endless work began to feel like rooted leadership, bearing fruit even in challenging seasons.

Leadership Rule of Life Checklist

1. **Prayer**: Do you set aside daily time for prayerful stillness?
2. **Sabbath**: Do you honor regular rhythms of rest and renewal?
3. **Reflection**: Do you pause weekly to notice God's presence in your leadership?
4. **Discernment**: Does your board have shared practices of listening and prayer?
5. **Renewal**: Do you revisit your rule of life quarterly, adjusting for the season?

A downloadable version of this checklist, with guiding questions, is available through the Effective Church Leadership Community (ECLC).

Suggested Practices

- Share your personal rule of life with the board as testimony and encouragement.
- Dedicate time at retreats to review or create a board rule of life.
- Encourage leaders to care for their bodies, spirits, and relationships as sacred trusts.
- Revisit Psalm 1 as a guiding text, reminding the board that fruit flows from rootedness.

Closing

"A rule of life roots leadership in God's steady rhythm."

Your leadership will be sustained not by constant striving but by rhythms that keep you rooted. By cultivating a rule of life—for yourself and for the board—you ensure that discernment flows steadily, energy is renewed, and the church bears fruit in season.

Discernment Prompts

- How does your current rhythm of life sustain—or drain—your leadership?
- What practices could be added or deepened to anchor you more fully in God?
- How might your board create a shared rule of life to steady its discernment?

Like roots seeking deeper soil and streams sustaining steady rhythms, a rule of life grounds your leadership, ensuring that the Spirit's fruit will flourish across every season.

Rooted for the Future

"Then the Lord answered me and said, Write a vision, and make it plain upon a tablet so that a runner can read it. There is still a vision for the appointed time; it testifies to the end; it does not deceive. If it delays, wait for it; for it is surely coming; it will not be late."

-Habakkuk 2:2–3 (CEB)

Opening Reflection

Roots stretch toward tomorrow even as they remain grounded in today. Streams carry life forward, nourishing fields that have not yet been planted. So too, leadership that is rooted in the Spirit must not only attend to the present but also prepare for the future.

As chairperson, you are entrusted with helping the board lift its eyes beyond today's tasks to discern God's unfolding vision. Habakkuk reminds us that the vision of God has its appointed time. Though it may feel slow in coming, it will not deceive. Your leadership is to help the board trust that God is already preparing tomorrow, even when today feels uncertain. To be rooted for the future is to plant seeds of hope now, trusting that the Spirit will water and grow them in God's time.

Suggested Practices

- Pray regularly for the church's future, not just its present needs.
- Dedicate time in meetings to imagine what God may be calling the church to five or ten years ahead.
- Invite the board to revisit the church's vision statement annually.
- Encourage patient trust, reminding the board that God's vision does not deceive.

Theological Framing

In *Embracing Our Call*, Chapter 17, we are reminded that vision is not about predicting trends but discerning where the Spirit is leading. Visionary leadership is an act of faith—it requires trust that God is already at work shaping tomorrow.

The **Calling–Energy–Resources–Discernment (CERD)** framework grounds this visionary task:

- **Calling**: The future must always align with God's calling for the church. Vision is not about novelty but about deeper faithfulness.
- **Energy**: Vision requires sustained energy. Leaders must pace themselves and nurture hope, ensuring the board does not grow weary in waiting.
- **Resources**: Preparing for the future includes stewarding resources today so that tomorrow's mission is possible. Wise investment, faithful budgets, and leadership development are all future-rooted practices.
- **Discernment**: Vision is clarified through prayerful discernment, not hurried planning. Listening for God's voice is the chairperson's greatest gift to the board's future work.

Your leadership ensures that the board is not consumed by the urgency of the present but remains attentive to the Spirit's unfolding tomorrow.

Suggested Practices

- Use CERD questions to guide annual visioning sessions.
- Reframe budget discussions as opportunities to invest in future mission.
- Encourage board members to see themselves as stewards of both present and future.
- Create space for silence in visioning work, trusting the Spirit to speak.

Case Study and Practical Steps

A church governing body faced dwindling attendance and financial pressures. Some members insisted the board should focus only on "keeping the lights on." Yet the chairperson sensed that God was calling the board to lift its eyes higher.

At a retreat, the chair read Habakkuk 2:2–3 and asked, "What vision might God be writing for us today that will shape tomorrow?" The group entered a time of prayer and silence. They then began to share images and hopes: a church alive in community service, worship that welcomed young families, partnerships with local schools. Though their present felt fragile, these visions stirred new energy.

The board developed a *Vision Discernment Guide* to help focus their work:

1. **Listen**: Begin every visioning session with silence and prayer.
2. **Name**: Record hopes and images that emerge, no matter how bold.
3. **Test**: Ask CERD questions—how does this align with calling, sustain energy, steward resources, invite discernment?
4. **Act**: Identify one small step to embody the vision now.
5. **Revisit**: Review and refresh the vision each year.

Over time, the board began reshaping its budget and energy to align with the vision. The congregation noticed renewed hope. What once felt like decline became the soil for Spirit-led renewal.

A downloadable version of the *Vision Discernment Guide*, with facilitation prompts, is available through the Effective Church Leadership Community (ECLC). Joining ECLC also provides access to webinars, resources, and templates to help boards remain rooted for the future.

Suggested Practices

- Schedule an annual vision retreat with your board.
- Encourage the congregation to pray for God's future call during worship.
- Share stories of hope, no matter how small, to build trust in God's unfolding work.
- Keep a written record of the board's visioning, returning to it each year.

Closing

"Rooted in the Spirit, your leadership sows hope for tomorrow."

As chairperson, you are called not only to guide today but to prepare the soil for tomorrow. Visionary leadership is patient, prayerful, and Spirit-led. It does not rush but trusts that God's vision has its appointed time.

Discernment Prompts

- How is God shaping your board's vision for the future?
- What seeds of hope can you plant now that may bear fruit in seasons to come?
- How can you help the board trust God's timing, even when vision feels delayed?

Like roots stretching toward tomorrow and streams carrying hope forward, your leadership ensures that the church remains grounded in God's call and prepared for the Spirit's unfolding future.

Conclusion

The roots have been planted.

Throughout this book, you have walked through practices, reflections, and stories meant to steady you in the sacred role of chairperson. We began by naming your call as the Mission Keeper—the one who helps ensure that the church's calling is discerned and that all of its energy and resources are faithfully directed toward it. Along the way, we explored how agendas, dialogue, policies, rhythms, crises, and even succession are all part of that task. Each chapter has offered tools to remind you that chairing is not only about keeping order—it is about keeping mission.

This is holy work.

You may never receive public recognition for it. Congregants may not know how much prayer, preparation, and discernment you invest before a meeting begins. Some may never notice how you pause in silence before a difficult vote, or how you reframe a tense discussion by returning to the church's mission statement. But the Spirit notices. And the body feels it, even when it cannot name it. Your leadership creates the soil in which calling takes root, grows strong, and bears fruit.

As chair, you are part of a partnership that holds the whole body steady. The pastor serves as Vision Driver, pointing the church toward God's unfolding future. The treasurer serves as Mission Interpreter, translating financial realities into stories of faithfulness. You serve as Mission Keeper, ensuring that all remains rooted in calling. Together, this partnership sustains the body, like intertwined roots drawing life from the same stream.

This book has not given you formulas to follow but practices to embody. You have been invited to:

Pray over agendas so that meetings flow toward calling.

Foster dialogue that invites the Spirit's presence.

Translate policies into practices that bear fruit.

Guide the board through seasons of the year, times of crisis, and moments of change.

Mentor successors, nurture unity, and cultivate a rule of life that sustains discernment.

These practices are not checkboxes to complete; they are rhythms to live. They are ways of leading that root your service in God's Spirit and remind the board that its true purpose is not to manage an organization but to embody Christ's mission.

As you conclude this book, I encourage you to pause for a moment of gratitude. Give thanks for those who have chaired before you—for their steadiness and faith. Give thanks for those who serve alongside you now—for pastors, treasurers, and fellow board members who share this responsibility. And give thanks for those who will chair after you, who even now may be quietly watching and learning from your example.

Leadership is always for a season. Your time as chair will not last forever, and it is not meant to. But the roots you help plant, the rhythms you help nurture, and the clarity you help sustain will endure beyond your term. Succession itself is part of your calling, for Spirit-led leadership always prepares the soil for tomorrow's growth.

And so, take heart. You are not alone in this role. You are part of a larger body, a broader tradition, and a living stream of leaders across time who have sought to guide God's people with faithfulness. The Spirit who called you to this work will sustain you in it.

"Rooted in the Spirit, your leadership sows hope for tomorrow."

As you go forward, may you be strengthened to keep mission at the center, to nurture dialogue that leads to unity, and to listen always for the Spirit's quiet whisper. May your leadership be like roots seeking deep water and like branches stretching toward the light—steady, grounded, and ever open to the growth God brings.

And may you know, in every meeting and every moment of service, that you are not simply managing a role but embodying a calling. You are the Mission Keeper. And through you, the church is steadied, guided, and prepared to bear fruit for God's kingdom.

10 Practices of Spirit-Led Chairing

As chairperson, you are entrusted with a sacred calling—not simply to manage meetings but to guide your board in Spirit-led discernment. These practices, drawn from the chapters of *Rooted in the Call*, offer a rhythm of leadership rooted in prayer, calling, and collaboration. Like streams that nourish soil and roots that anchor trees, these practices sustain your leadership across seasons. Each is tied to a chapter in this book, and together they form a living guide. For further resources, tools, and templates, explore the Effective Church Leadership Community (ECLC), where these practices are deepened and shared.

1. Honor Your Sacred Placement (Chapter 1)
Remember that you are planted by the Spirit for this season. Ground your leadership in God's calling, trusting that your placement is not random but purposeful. CERD reminds you that calling shapes all else.

2. Root Your Identity in God's Call (Chapter 2)
Your identity as chair is not in tasks but in Spirit-led stewardship. Reflect weekly on how your roots are nourished by calling, energy, resources, and discernment. This grounding steadies you.

3. Pray Over Agendas (Chapter 3)
Agendas are more than lists; they shape how the board listens to God. Pray over each agenda, placing discernment before routine reports, ensuring every meeting flows toward calling.

4. Cultivate a Listening Posture (Chapter 4)
Listening is leadership. Begin meetings with silence, creating space for the Spirit's whisper. Discernment emerges when energy is slowed, and hearts are open.

5. Foster Dialogue That Builds Unity (Chapter 5)
Facilitate dialogue as a sacred practice. Encourage open-hearted sharing, guiding the board to discern together rather than debate apart. Unity is woven through listening and patience.

6. Translate Policy into Practice (Chapter 6)
Policies are trellises for mission. Guide the board in aligning policies with calling, ensuring they bear fruit in daily ministry. Steward resources with integrity and clarity.

7. Lead with Seasonal Rhythm (Chapter 7)
Anchor the board in an annual rhythm of discernment. Name the season—planting, tending, harvesting, or resting—and guide practices that align with God's appointed times.

8. Nurture the Whole Body (Chapter 8)
Leadership is about collaboration. Strengthen the partnership of

board, pastor, and congregation, ensuring each part of the body is honored, connected, and nourished by calling.

9. Steady the Board in Crisis (Chapter 9)
In storms, guide the board toward prayerful patience. Use CERD to frame decisions in calling and resources, helping the church find resilience rooted in God's enduring presence.

10. Plant Seeds for the Future (Chapters 10–12)
Succession, rhythm, and vision are seeds for tomorrow. Mentor successors, shape a rule of life for sustainability, and invite the board to dream with God's vision in mind. Leadership is faithful when it prepares the soil for future fruit.

These ten practices are not a checklist but a living rhythm. As you return to them, may your leadership remain rooted in God's Spirit, bearing fruit that nourishes the church for years to come.

Scripture Index

Scripture Reference	Translation	Page
1 Kings 19:11–12	CEV	29
Psalm 1:3	TLB	75
Proverbs 11:1	CEB	43
Proverbs 16:3	MSG	23
Ecclesiastes 3:1	NIV	49
Habakkuk 2:2–3	CEB	81
Matthew 18:20	TLB	35
Romans 5:3–5	MSG	63
1 Corinthians 12:18	NIV	9
1 Corinthians 12:26	CEV	55
Ephesians 4:16	CEB	15
2 Timothy 2:2	CEV	69

Effective Church Leadership Community

Equipping Leaders to Serve Faithfully, Lead Boldly, and Follow the Spirit Together

Leadership in the church is sacred, courageous work. You don't have to do it alone.

The Effective Church Leadership Community is a free online space for pastors, treasurers, board members, and ministry leaders to connect, grow, and lead with clarity. Through webinars, tools, best practices, and supportive conversation, we help churches align energy and resources with God's calling — not alone, but together.

Whether you're stepping into leadership or guiding others, this community offers practical wisdom and spiritual encouragement for the road ahead.

Scan to join or visit the link below:

https://community.churchtrainingcenter.com

Continue the Journey

Your work as chairperson is part of a larger stream of Spirit-led leadership. Just as roots are nourished by surrounding soil, your leadership is enriched when supported by companions along the way. The following resources complement *Rooted in the Call*, providing depth, tools, and practices that sustain your service. Together they form a library of wisdom, each one strengthening your ability to guide the board with clarity, discernment, and hope. For further resources and templates, the Effective Church Leadership Community (ECLC) offers expanded support.

Sacred Listening: Discovering God's Call for Your Life
This devotional guide invites you into practices of silence, prayer, and discernment. It equips you to cultivate listening in your own life and to foster a board culture that waits upon the Spirit before acting.

Embracing Our Call: A Practical Guide for Church Governing Body Leaders
This is the foundational textbook for Spirit-led governance. It helps you anchor your leadership in the Calling–Energy–Resources–Discernment framework, ensuring that the entire board aligns structure and mission.

Called Together: A Spirit-Led Discernment Guide for Congregational Planning
This guide offers nine phases of planning grounded in prayer and discernment. It supports your leadership by giving the congregation a shared process for shaping vision and mission faithfully.

Serving the Call: A Training Manual for New Governance Body Members
This workbook provides practical exercises, templates, and examples to orient new board members. It strengthens your chairing by offering tools to train and equip others for Spirit-led governance.

The Ministry of Money: A Treasurer's Role in the Mission of the Church
This book reframes the treasurer's work as a sacred ministry. It complements your leadership by ensuring that stewardship of money remains aligned with calling and mission, freeing you to guide with confidence.

The Heart of Stewardship: The Practice of Faith
This workbook companion to *The Ministry of Money* offers practical tools for treasurers and finance committees. It reinforces your leadership by ensuring that financial stewardship is practiced with integrity and faith, bridging policy and mission.

A Final Word

As you rise from these pages and return to the work entrusted to you, remember: you are not alone. The Spirit who called you into leadership will sustain you through every meeting, every conversation, and every season of service.

Stay rooted in prayer. Keep watch over the mission with courage and humility. Trust that God's vision will unfold in its time. And when challenges bend you low, know that roots grow deepest in storms, drawing strength from hidden streams.

Your leadership matters. Your quiet faithfulness shapes the board, steadies the church, and prepares the way for fruit you may never see.

Go forward with gratitude and trust, carrying this truth: **you are the Mission Keeper, and the Spirit is your guide.**

www.ingramcontent.com/pod-product-compliance
Lightning Source LLC
Chambersburg PA
CBHW032235080426
42735CB00008B/867